The 30-Day Challenge

A Freelancer's Guide to Making $1,000 in Your First Month to a Six-Figure Income in a Year!

By

Sylvia Powell

Copyright © 2019 – *CSBA Publishing House*

Email:csbapublishing@gmail.com

All Rights Reserved.

No part of this publication may be reproduced, stored in a retrieval system or transmitted in any form or by any means, electronic, mechanical, photocopying, recording or otherwise without the proper written consent of the copyright holder, except brief quotations used in a review.

Published by:

CSBA Publishing

CSBA Publishing House
Cover & Interior designed

By

Renee Robson

First Edition

Contents

My Story 8

What is Freelancing? 23

Who Can Become a Freelancer? 32

    Factors for Success 35

        Stay Focused. 35

        Stay Self-Disciplined. 36

        Stay Organized. 37

        Manage Time Well. 38

        Stay Motivated. 41

        Deliver Well. 42

Finding and Polishing Your Skills 45

    Define Your Skills. 45

    Ways to Find Jobs 48

Freelancing Fields 53

    Computers and Information Systems(IT) 53

    Administrative 54

    Finance 55

    Customer Service 55

Writing 56

Education 56

Public Relations Consultant 57

Transcriber 57

Graphic Designer... 57

Virtual Assistant 58

Travel Consulting 58

Accounting 58

Online Researcher 59

Editing.. 59

Social Media Management 60

Getting Started 61

   Job Marketplaces... 63

      SolidGigs.. 63

      Fiverr 63

      Upwork 64

      CloudPeeps 64

      Indeed 65

      College Recruiter.. 65

Freelancer	65
Guru	66
ServiceScape	66
Craigslist	66
Getting Paid	67
PayPal	67
Payoneer	69
How to Draw Attention	72
Create a Winning Profile	73
Get Straight to the Point	73
Answer Question Words	73
Be Concise, Yet Thorough	74
It's a Resume	74
Use a Professional Picture	74
Update as Needed	75
Connect the Personal	76
Charge Fairly	76
Don't Undercharge	76
Don't Overcharge	77

The 30 Day Challenge 78

    Examine Your Worth 78

    Reach Out 79

        Word of Mouth is Gold 80

        Network 81

    Be Personal 82

    Other Tips for a Successful Challenge 83

        Set up Google alerts. 85

        Remain in constant communication with your clients. 85

        Always be on the lookout for freelancing business. 85

        Chronicle your social media links. 85

        Ask for kind words. 86

        Stay in the know. 86

        Image is everything. 87

        Perfect your niche. 87

        Involve yourself with coworking spaces 88

        Consider freebies. 88

        Engagement is key. 89

Buy ads. 89

Write for niche publications. 90

Carefully negotiate. 90

Adjust your prices. 91

Set boundaries. 91

Communication advice. 92

Finance matters. 94

Establish a designated workplace. 95

Time management skills. 96

Find mentors. 97

Get insurance. 97

Conclusion 99

My Story

With a mission in mind, earning a 6-figure income as a freelancer is very possible.

Attaining this goal takes careful planning, applying proven strategies, and relentlessness.

I had pitched so much almost every day that one of my friends called me "relentless." I felt compelled to find out its definition and see if I matched up with what these professionals thought I was all about.

The dictionary defines the word "relentless" as persistent and unyielding. I could live with that, and so can you as a freelancer.

I will share my freelancing journey with you to give you an example of how to earn more money from your talent and to expand on it in several areas.

I believed it when my parents told me that I was sitting on a million bucks and didn't even know it.

My parents were always talking in parables when I was a kid. I can stake my life on the fact that this was a saying handed down to them through generations.

I didn't know it then, but it was a sure sign of things to come. I pondered over their affirmation many a day, especially when I was in a financial rut. Unfortunately, this was more often than not in my early days as a freelancer.

Part of the challenge derived from the fact that I was not taught to be a business owner. My generation was taught to get an education or trade and then get a well-paying, stable job, respectively.

Then, I decided to dissect the words of the allegory. To me, it meant that I had the internal makings and drive to earn lots of money.

My first inkling to try to see if these words had any truth to them came when the place where I worked abruptly closed. I had no idea what to do. I had to dig deep.

I came up with a plan to contact everybody I had come into contact with over the years and explain that I was looking to start my own editorial venture. They knew I could write, I was personable, and I had a slew of media contacts.

These three attributes that I acquired over the years were sure to win them over. And fortunately, it did. Lawyers, doctors, politicians, small businesses, politicians, department heads, and individuals wanted a piece of the action.

My mind was going in a million areas and landed on a lesson I'd learned many years ago in a marketing class.

One-third of every list of contacts will more than likely become a sale. This was the law of marketing. This was the answer.

Make a list of potential customers. Once the contract is landed, subtly ask for referrals and any incentive you could offer for them for providing the referrals.

Marketing yourself and your freelance business may appear to become cumbersome. But you must keep at it with the same vigor as when you came up with the idea to start freelancing in the first place.

Every day, I made contact with at least 50 people or companies in my circle and the referrals from their circle. I went to their parties, meetings, and gatherings. I made them a promise that I could increase their bottom line through media-generated marketing by getting them some press in newspapers, radio programs, or television stations.

I came to the revelation that people are vain by nature. They love to "toot their own horn" so to speak. I played on this character flaw and used it to my advantage.

My communication with them always involved the praises they would receive hiring me to put them in the limelight. Customers didn't want to admit this opening, but I knew secretly that it was exactly what they craved.

Start early. The old adage, "the early bird catches the worm," rings true in this instance. Getting to potential clients early before they have had time to get bogged down with their day gives a freelancer an added advantage over the competition.

I put my game face on. For each potential client, I came up with a list of people, organizations, and companies that would benefit from their offerings.

I did all their back-office duties, posters, flyers, press releases, public service announcements, trade mentions, and specialty media - all in the name of getting my clients noticed.

Fortunately, it worked! Soon everything was a buzz.

Another thing I did was to join organizations that would be potential clients of mine like women's groups, small business groups, city fair committees, the city bazaar planning committee, and festivals. I did volunteer work for them for the mere mention of my name and my offerings.

I paraded these associations before my clients, and this gave me an advantage over the competition. I lunched with them, introduced myself to their members, bartered, and pitched any and every idea I could come up with to form a connection.

I signed up to offer free speeches on media-generated marketing to all the budding businesses in the city who attend the Department of Business Development training sessions in my hometown.

Each month, there were at least 50 or more eager attendees to these events sponsored by the city's business department. At each event, I talked afterward to the people, gave them my card, and referrals of past clients.

Again, according to the laws of marketing, one-third of the contacts would turn into a sale. This proved successful, and I began to think of other department agencies to contact.

Once I exhausted this list, I called on the veteran affairs office of the Small Business Administration. This was a large agency with plenty of clients who needed my services.

I knew this population would be eager to hear how they could start and operate a successful business with media-generated publicity. I would be doing a grave service to our veterans who had served our country.

I attended their meetings and asked for a few moments to speak to the crowd. Again, I spoke to them individually after the meeting and gave my sales pitch. Besides making contacts, attending speaking engagements proved valuable as well.

Once I joined these groups, I was allowed to have my offerings placed in their newsletters, with my contact information and my sales pitch, for free. People started contacting me for a consultation, and I gave it to them.

I had a lawyer associate who was actually another freelancer's potential client. She had just mentioned him to me and said he was recently fired from the firm where he worked.

I met with him, and he said over and over again that he did not have any money and didn't know what he was going to do. He had nowhere to turn, he said. I offered him a way out of his situation.

Deep down inside, I knew that he knew a lot of people, and I would make money through his connections. My freelancing marketing services came in handy. I told him to hold off on paying me anything, just give me a chance to show him that all was not lost in his dilemma.

I did, and before you know it, I was handling all of his speaking engagements to set up businesses for people who were interested in taking the plunge of business ownership. They all needed his legal expertise.

I happened to look at the piles of paper spread out over his desk one day and asked if I could help him organize them. He said he simply did not have the time to return the calls or correspondence to the people who had inquired.

I offered to do this task for him and free up his time. The majority of these people ultimately scheduled appointments with him or simply had a phone consultation. Many paid him a setup fee to start their businesses, and the money started to pour in without him ever leaving his office.

These businesses who became his clients also needed editorial work like brochures, business plans, marketing plans, and website copy. This is what is called a win-win situation at its best.

From then on, I met the lawyer at restaurants, his office, over coffee breaks, early mornings, and late evenings. He became my greatest fan for years to come. He also proved a great candidate for spreading the word about my freelancing services.

In another instance, two of the attendees from one of my speaking engagements invited me to their church. This was not just any usual church, but a mega-church of over 5,000 people.

The members were looking for a keynote speaker for an upcoming event and would pay handsomely. I eventually accepted. The ministry paid me, and I landed several private clients who were interested in my services.

One of the clients from the church was a long-standing member of a group that needed editorial work done for their pamphlet for their yearly fundraising event. Yes, I signed them up for my service, too.

All the while, I am still making contacts, going to meetings that my niche audience attends, going to functions, and being seen and heard.

I decided, after I had garnered a large number of customers, to host my own event. I would teach budding businesses how to get started in marketing. I held the group in a neighborhood restaurant every Tuesday.

The event was quite successful. The people who attended ordered food and drinks. The restaurant received money, and so did I.

Another great strategy is to connect to a nonprofit organization that is in your niche.

For example, if you are a computer wizard, help inner-city kids or boys' and girls' clubs with computer literacy. You could even go to a school that needs someone to teach about these areas.

Corporations and governments typically fund these types of

activities for nonprofits. Thus, you are building another layer on your contact list. Something may even emerge from these activities that you hadn't thought of already.

At first glance, you would probably ask yourself why in the world you would volunteer your valuable time and effort for free. Because those people know people. And those people they know, know other people. There is an instant network among those ranks.

I once met with a writing group every Saturday. These people would come to the class, eager to learn more about the craft from an expert. I gave them that insight. Each participant paid a nominal fee, and I left them fulfilled while I earned some pocket change to fuel next week's workload.

This is also an excellent way to get press. The media has a large audience of loyal readers. Invite a journalist for a visit to your groups and put your shine on.

Once the news hits the press, readers will become interested and tell other people. At the end of the day, you are getting the word out about yourself and your expertise in your niche.

By chance, I met someone with an international organization that had worked tirelessly to build her group over the years. I heard through the grapevine that she knew everybody.

She became a jewel in spreading the word about my service within her group members and constituents. I offered discounts to her members as an added benefit for them joining her group.

I carved out a niche in her group as the writing consultant for all editorial work needed by its members.

Those people know people who know other people.

It's a cycle that goes as far as you want to take it.

I sent out introductory letters to all her members and my contact information with little anecdotes to common writing challenges.

Each newsletter, I would give much-needed advice to potential authors, business owners, organization start-ups, business plans, marketing plans, magazine ideas, newsletters, and other marketing material.

I purchased a blog that focused on teaching English to people in other countries.

This is typically known as English as a Second Language (ESL).

The name of the website was called Learn English 247.com.

As the CEO of this venture, my duties included:

- Overseeing the overall day-to-day management and operations of the business

- Procuring student contacts

- Writing ads to promote the website on several platforms

- Soliciting other teachers to come on board under my leadership

- Writing press releases and broadcast material

- Developed visual campaigns tailored to my company

Because I was a freelance writer, I farmed out my work to just about every publication I could think of locally, statewide, and throughout the country. I extended my talent by offering grant writing and media relations consulting for small businesses, start-ups, and individuals.

I would write business plans, public relations plans, marketing plans, and proposals. Writing taught me how to become an expert at proofreading, editing, and researching, and I added those elements to my list as well.

I was once a book publisher and worked on different author's marketing and public relations plans. Some of the magazines I worked with included business publications doing profiles of local entrepreneurs, new products, and reviews.

I served as a communications and publishing consultant for universities and the Redevelopment and Housing Authorities editing, writing, and proofing their communications with residents. The housing authorities also needed someone to speak to the residents on various topics, and I did that too.

You can just imagine how wide the door of opportunity opened with the coming of the digital age. It has increased a hundredfold with publications cropping up daily.

If you follow this script, a freelancer could easily make a six-figure income in no time. Repeat these strategies mentioned above repeatedly. You will see the increase in your bottom line.

In the beginning chapters of the book, I explore the decision to take the leap of faith and pursue going solo. Various aspects of freelancing are discussed to give a more comprehensive view of what it is and what it involves.

Important issues are considered, such as leaving traditional full-time employment while testing the waters in the freelancing arena either part-time or on a full-time basis.

Is there enough money to live on while building your new-found freelancing career? Are you able to handle isolation for long periods while you work?

Remaining persistent and relentless in your quest to become a successful freelancer will give you staying power.

What is Freelancing?

The face of America's workforce is changing rapidly. Freelancing, or side hustles, have become the new labor force driving the economic wheel. Many freelancers earn a good, honest living doing this type of work.

Don't let that gut feeling steer you in the wrong direction or take you off course. In business, the keywords are usually "location, location, location." In the realm of freelancing and becoming your own boss, the keywords are "plan, plan, plan." Have everything lined up in advance before you attempt to make the first sale.

Have a system in place to cover late checks, bounced checks, and underpaid checks. Think about the worst-case scenarios as you build your reputation among your target audience of potential customers. This tested system comes in handy.

According to the Freelance Industry Report, almost half of freelancers are writers, 18% writing full-time, 10% editing/copy-editing, 10% copywriting, 20% as designers, translators 8%, web designers 5.5%, and marketing 4%.

Freelancers make up nearly 40% of the United States workforce, currently.

Do the math. If a freelancer gets X number of customers at an average $35 an hour, that adds up to a hefty amount of change. For me, everybody I encountered was a potential customer, and I was ready to sell them on my service.

However, rewarding the experience may be, freelancing is a risky business. Payments can be inconsistent, unexpected charges may occur while conducting your business, and staying on top of tax requirements is crucial.

Let's be real for a moment. Everything in this world centers around money. It's what makes the world go around.

Working for yourself is a dream for many, and freelancing could be the answer. The flexibility and control it offers present endless opportunities.

So, what is freelancing?

Well, to eke out a definition, freelancing involves work performed on a contractual basis for a certain agreed-upon price for a certain agreed-upon service. In a nutshell, freelancing is basically a form of self-employment. Freelancing is a conscious way of earning money from a client or company. It's quite different from waiting on the anticipated paycheck every Friday.

In this case, the freelancer controls every aspect of wage earnings, frequency, and duration. It means doing away with the 9 to 5 grind, the boss, and charting an independent course.

The freelancer becomes his own boss.

The good news is you are not alone on the freelancer journey. An estimated 57 million people made the same choice in 2018. That number is expected to triple by the year 2020, according to the most available labor statistics.

Some wage-earners perform side work on a part-time basis as a way of making extra dollars on the side that can eventually turn into a full-time gig.

There are some perks to freelancing. Naming your price for time spent on duties and the money to be made is endless.

It may be time to start tooting your own horn for a change. But be careful. This is only for the brave at heart and those who are fully committed to this venture.

Freelancers have made a firm commitment to stick it out despite the challenges that may arise. They enter into an open labor market by choosing an alternative way of earning a living.

Convincing potential customers that you are the best choice to do the work is key. More often than not, potential freelancers have been able to cultivate a small customer list before officially turning in their resignation letters at their full-time jobs.

Many leave the brick-and-mortar buildings and work from home in their home office, meeting clients at coffee shops, quiet restaurants, and libraries. Freelancers are free to work just about anywhere, but most choose to work from home. If the client has an office, freelancers can meet there to hash out the details and sign the contract.

Pursuing other avenues to earn a living is attractive to many these days. Juggling work and family life become a breeze.

Freelancing is work, though. It's an alternative form of labor, but even so, it remains work - getting paid to perform a specified duty.

Instead of working for a company, freelancers go out and seek work from several avenues. Potential companies or client's contract with you to perform a given task.

Often, freelancers work with several companies on a variety of projects. Like working for yourself, the freelancer pays their own taxes, keeping track of their time and labor.

Usually, if an employee has performed certain duties for a long period or has a talent or skill, they are a candidate for becoming a freelancer. In other words, anyone can easily become a freelancer.

People in fields that can typically work as freelancers include:

- Virtual assistants

- Writers

- Information technology (IT) contractors

- Editors

- Proofreaders

- Business consultants

All that is needed is a skill that clients find valuable and are willing to pay good money for.

Evaluate what your strengths are. Then, ask yourself how many people would be willing to pay for this service.

Freelancers can earn anywhere from $10 to $75 as the going rate per hour. For specific industry niches, like tech-related fields, language translators, and teachers, those numbers can go even higher.

A vital element to taking the plunge into independent living, free of having another person dictate your schedule, is having enough money to fall back on until the checks start rolling in regularly.

Even the savviest freelancer may hit this roadblock a time or two on their journey.

Don't get left holding the bag when rent, car payments, and the mortgage comes due. Align your dreams with your work-flow plans.

Testing the waters on your freelancing venture is the best option. Perhaps diving into this on a part-time basis while you still have gainful employment may be the best choice.

Be realistic. Don't let your emotions get in the way of rational decision-making.

Don't let your dreams doom your plans from the start while neglecting your personal responsibilities at home. Dreams have a way of sometimes taking over rational thinking.

But, if the freelancing dream is still your heart's desire, then go for it. Keep all the nay-sayers at bay who criticize your choice.

There are some people, however, who will applaud you for having the courage and dedication to do something you've always wanted to do: To be your own boss.

All in all, freelancing can be a lucrative venture. Stay focused. It can happen.

You must believe this notion or failure is just around the corner.

Freelancing can also be a dream come true or your worst nightmare. Think before you leap.

Another caveat is to prepare for the unexpected.

Dealing with the blow of possible disappointments determines coming out of it successfully intact without collateral damage.

While freelancing may be rewarding, it is equally as trying and challenging.

Who Can Become a Freelancer?

Just about anyone can become a freelancer with virtually very little experience. That means, if you have a skill from previous or current work or hobby that you perform, you can freelance.

The length of time and the knowledge you've been able to cultivate only gives you an edge over the competition.

Traditional workplace environments are fading, and employees are looking to hone their skills and talent to try their hand at freelancing.

By choice or by necessity, dreams of being self-employed occur every day. Sometimes, a change in work schedules, lowered pay grades, family illness, layoffs, a change in family dynamics necessitates this decision.

Either way, it's an open field for virtually anyone with time, skill, or talent to make their mark.

The notion that one must have a degree to start freelancing is untrue. Many freelancers out there are successful without receiving a formal education.

If this applies to you, then you are a prime candidate to becoming a freelancer. Some formal work experience in the field is a plus. This allows for a greater advantage to sell yourself to potential clients.

Competition can be fierce, even in independent arenas. Being educated and skilled in your craft only boosts your chances of landing more clients and referrals.

With that being said, the truth of the matter is that working hard to obtain clients and maintaining a clean reputation goes a long way in sustaining and growing your freelancing career.

Some freelancers begin their freelance careers straight out of college or after years of practicing their craft on a job.

A survey of 3,000 professionals revealed that nearly 44% of those employees were interested in freelance work. The schedule appealed to them, with 26% of that number already serving as freelancers.

In this same study, parents were asked their opinions on balancing work and family-life in their choice of career. The flexibility of work came out as the top answer with 1,200 parents who had children age 18 and younger living at home. That coupled with the fact that 26% of households are led by single parents who work full-time.

For the most part, freelancing could turn into a full-time career. Whether you start out intermittently doing it to earn some side money or begin this feat on a larger scale. Either way, if done right, it can bring you freedom.

Factors for Success

Do you have a skill that everyone can perform? Do you have a skill and ability that others admire and separate you from the rest?

Freelancing requires more than just skill sets. It encompasses setting goals, planning well, and being diligent in seeking out projects.

Some sound advice before you sink your teeth into this idea would be to talk to other people who are maintaining careers in this fashion. This would be a prime opportunity to find out first-hand from a reliable source if freelancing is something you really want to do or not.

There are five major points to starting and maintaining a lucrative freelancing career.

Stay Focused.

There is going to come a time or times in the freelancer's life that concentration and attention are required to complete and work on an agreed-upon project.

This verbal or written alliance between you and the client speaks volumes as it develops trust, establishes any dependence concerns, and answers any reliance questions within the business relationship.

At some point, the freelancer will have to tell friends, family, and those they hold near-and-dear, "no." Responding in this fashion strengthens your commitment to conquering the task at hand.

A big myth that those not freelancers have is that you work at home and sit around the house all day. Quite the contrary, freelancers need and require quiet, undisturbed time to finish a job correctly. Staying focused allows the freelancer to concentrate without disruption on completing work on time.

Stay Self-Disciplined.

The dictionary defines self-disciple as the ability to control and motivate yourself and staying on track without enlisting the help of others

An equally critical area for the freelancer is to develop the skill of controlling yourself to do the necessary things. In this case, the project for your client.

To have a stable freelancing career, hold yourself accountable to complete the list of things that are important for the client. This is what you cling to when you are tempted to stray away from a designated goal.

Self-discipline is a major trait that should be at the top of the list to have a stable freelancing career. Self-governing your time and the amount of time that you do it is the very backbone of business success.

Maintain your efforts on a single task at a time so as not to get overwhelmed. Try to avoid distractions stop or hinder you from working

Anything or anyone outside of your parameter of duties is a distraction that only serves as annoyances. Train yourself to see the job to its completion.

This will make you work smarter, not harder.

Stay Organized.

Even the smallest of things have the potential to throw a perfectly built plan into disarray. Keeping all working material in one location saves time in searching for items to complete your project on time.

Make sure that you have gathered all the materials needed to complete the project and that they are within arm's reach. Look for things that eat away at your available time and break up a smooth workflow.

Choose an area in the house that only you frequent, and that way, things are exactly where you place them and can retrieve them when needed. Spending hours upon hours trying to pinpoint where you left something steals time away from you and the project.

Removing the clutter from your work area creates a certain peace and calmness as you go about fine-tuning your client's job. It can sometimes be a challenge to overlook the piles of accumulated paper or boxes stacked on top of one another.

When something is lost, it is exhausting attempting to figure out where was the elusive last place you saw it. Keep everything in check to the best of your ability. It goes a long way.

Manage Time Well.

Being able to manage your time means you can complete work and meet designated deadlines. Freelancers can sometimes get overburdened with projects and have extended themselves because of the extra time required to do them.

Having good time-management skills is a must. It's a characteristic that almost barricades a person into certain parameters to stay time managed.

This is particularly true for freelancers who often are juggling work with other time-sensitive things like family and play. Taking a breather from working on the project means allowing for a designated amount of time to pass before getting back on the job.

The adage that "practice makes perfect" could apply here. This technique is something that you consciously force yourself to do until it becomes natural.

Start monitoring yourself and how long it takes to do a particular task or action. Then, ask yourself how you could have performed the action in less time if you wanted to.

Developing good time-management skills means looking at yourself in a way you never have before. While it can be a bit daunting for some, it is a doable task.

Take a day or two or even a week and experiment with doing activities in a more efficient, shorter amount of time while still completing them. At first, it may seem like a struggle, but each day, it gets easier and easier until you can do it with your eyes closed.

Even the smallest of things can eat away at your time. This primarily has to do with people in general who have a lot of things to do in the day and little time to do them.

A plan of action comes into play at this point. You can master the art of time management if you are committed and sincere about making a change in habits. As everybody knows, breaking long-time habits is difficult, but achievable.

Being your own boss and keeping tabs on yourself means self-governing virtually every single aspect of your day. Make a schedule that you can live with, then put things in order of priority. Distractions may happen, so have an action plan in place to tackle them at the beginning. Lastly, get to work, don't procrastinate.

Stay Motivated.

Freelancing is a lonely, solo practice. More than likely, you will be spending the better part of the day alone. Flying solo is almost always required. It is necessary to craft out your projects.

There won't be the sounds of the bullhorn along with cheering crowds of people chanting you forward. The decision to make a go of a freelancing career is your baby and yours alone.

Some freelancers feel isolated and lonely, working from home and away from a traditional workplace. Office chatter, conversations, and interactions are few and far between.

While working from home has its benefits, it can have its downside. Many freelancers miss the social aspect of work life. When these feelings arise, it usually begins to impact a person's motivation.

Join a group or network of other freelancers. Connecting with another human-being always helps to keep the blues away. Perhaps these associates can help obtain more contracts, offer some best practices in your field, or a comforting shoulder to openly discuss concerns.

Find a co-office environment where freelancers gather to discuss various aspects of their work and resources. Some offices rent out spaces for solo entrepreneurs, which comes with a secretary who handles all the back-office needs of these tenants. In this case, freelancers can remain independent and connected at the same time.

Attending networking events. These events are a good place to meet other like-minded people for friendship or camaraderie.

Social networking channels also offer a great means to reach out and touch people. Avenues like Twitter, Facebook, Instagram, and SnapChat can aid in staying informed, connected, and can help revive your motivation.

Deliver Well.

In the freelancing world, it is always a best practice to over-deliver and under commit.

This means that if an agreement is made with a client, provide a little more than discussed or promised.

Go the extra mile.

Make the customer feel important and special. This may be just the thing that lands you a long-term client.

If you tell a client you are going to do something, do it, and in the timeframe the client asks for.

Some things to keep in mind:

- Follow-though on all promises.

- Make sure you never promise anything unless you are sure you can make good on them.

- Only say yes to those things that you can ensure is carried out.

- It is okay to say No to a client. I wouldn't make this a habit, but it is better to do this than to break promises from being too eager for their business.

- Be as honest as possible. This builds trust if something is thrown in your work schedule that may take you away from a deadline. Don't make excuses. The truth works best every time.

These are the most fool-proof secrets to success for freelancers or contract workers. You don't want to skimp by in these areas because these measures improve credibility and client trust.

Finding and Polishing Your Skills

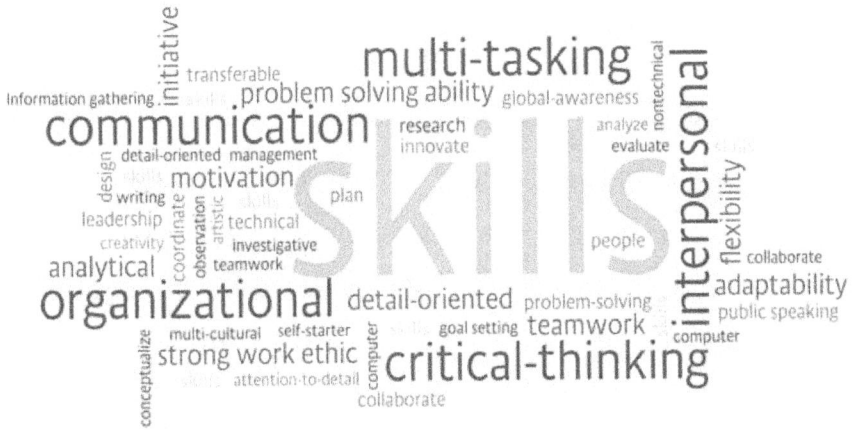

Operating a freelance enterprise or work-for-hire career requires a variety of skills.

Define Your Skills

Having a defined skill in a popular area which you learned at work while doing a hobby, or with innate gifts like cooking, typing, or art, means offering a valuable service to companies for pay. Identifying and refining your craft is essential to gaining reputation in the marketplace.

Take a moment to sincerely ask yourself what skills you have that you think someone would pay for. It could cooking, mechanical, IT, fashion, makeup, sewing, writing, or something of that nature.

Getting started with this question aids in determining what to do first in a freelancing career. Consider what strengths you have and put that upfront as you ponder on what you can do well.

Try asking family, friends, neighbors, or co-workers what their impression is of your talent. These people closest to you can help measure the worth of your talent.

Check your arsenal of skills and come up with at least 10 ideas on things where you have mastery, meaning those work-related tasks that you can perform well.

Finding your skill and homing in on your talent isn't easy for beginners. Select a talent that you do that you're passionate about. The old adage "do what you love, and the money will come" rings true in many instances here.

From there comes the hard work. Begin to research and formulate a list of potential jobs in the freelance realm that would be easy to transition into.

Also, think back on some of your initial employment history and select those duties that were assigned to you. Ask yourself: what are some duties, sills, workshops, and training you attended at those places?

With my first inclination to freelance, I wrote down all the jobs I'd had thus far, then picked out those attributes of the employment that I personally had a stake in carrying out. Once I did that, my skills list began to grow and develop into a strong, viable one.

In college, I tutored students in English, especially the ones from other countries where English was not their native tongue. I worked as a cook for the students who yearned for a homecooked meal. I remembered one time I had even worked as a data entry clerk at the University parttime. Years later, I worked at a newspaper as a customer service representative for subscriptions while writing on a freelance basis.

Ideas on fine-tuning your talent could include life-long learning courses or groups in your niche that offer classes or opportunities to add to your arsenal of works. These activities may seem small but carry a lot of weight in some circles. The world of work, particularly freelance work, is evolving every day.

Ways to Find Jobs

Once that's done, do a simple Google search for freelance websites and job boards to see what is currently in demand and what contractors are looking for. Several items may pique your interest.

The next thing that should be done is to create profiles on popular platforms like Upwork and Fiverr. These websites cater to freelancers in a variety of ways. You can also get an idea of what freelancing jobs are already on the market.

Then, it was almost as if I carried around a sign that read, "will travel for money." Being mobile in meeting with potential clients raised the stakes in my freelancing business. I went everywhere and anywhere to meet them on their turf or close by. I kept my walking shoes in the car and changed to my professional ones once I approached the mutually agreed upon meeting location.

While gathering my best practices in finding self-employment jobs, I came up with several ways to look for work and several methods in finding them.

I visited these places with my business cards in hand and ready-at-will samples that I would show to any willing party:

- Schools
- Universities
- City hall
- Government offices
- Community civic associations
- Housing residential teams
- Housing authorities
- Small business groups
- Organizations and meetings where my target audience attended

The workflow began to blossom.

One thing to keep in mind, be safe. While the effort to obtain stable, consistent clients is the focus, they are still strangers. Meet in public places where people are around and ensure from all referrals that these people are on the up and up.

Whatever your niche happens to be, there is a guarantee that someone is looking for it. Positioning yourself to capture those opportunities and drive them your way can make the difference between success or failure.

I had asked everyone in my circle to tell someone about their experience with me, and please give me referrals from friends, family, and colleagues. It took a lot of patience, but in the end, things began to flow favorably using this technique. I offered a discount on other work they wanted me to perform for taking a moment to give me the referrals.

Try gaining initial experience by working on projects for people you know. Warm sells include friends, family, and other colleagues you can call upon. Try your best sales pitch on for size with this receptive group.

Compile a list of entities, platforms, organizations, or companies that fit into that niche. It may be a small one to start but has the potential to grow once you get in front of them and sell yourself. Build a portfolio to present with references to vouch for your talent.

Try to come up with at least 10 target audiences. That is, sectors of the population who have similar things in common. These audiences could be doctors, lawyers, teachers, or any professional who could benefit from your services.

I know it may be a little unnerving to talk to others about yourself and what great services you offer, especially someone you never met before. But these cold sales could lead to some potential clients. Cold sales include everyone outside of your immediate circles, such as business organizations and individuals with whom you have no personal connection.

More and more companies are beginning to reach out to contract employees to provide a service or product. Opportunities arise all the time.

Collaborate with a more seasoned, experienced freelancer.

For example, I knew a graphics designer, and I worked closely with them on just about any project as a writer providing content.

It's okay to go solo, but be open to collaborative opportunities that may come your way.

Freelancing Fields

There is an endless array of freelancing opportunities out there if you know where to look.

To help jump-start your quest, here are a few popular industries that I came up where freelancing is common, but the choices are certainly not limited to these options.

Computers and Information Systems (IT)

This is one of the hottest sectors in the freelance world.

Just about every segment of business revolves around utilizing a computer. IT covers the gamut in terms of streamlining enterprise functions.

The days of pen and paper communications have become obsolete. Conversations are now moving to the digital age by necessity.

This type of job encompasses web-site design, maintenance, technical support, and cybersecurity. It could also include data entry, administrative tasks, or help desk technicians.

The ongoing rise in technology-related needs is in demand.

Administrative

Administrative jobs are crucial to ensuring that entities run seamlessly.

Duties could include typing, filing, records management, public relations, office manager, and administrative assistant.

A freelancer could serve as support staff to office operations or coordinator. Other tasks may be data processing or medical coding.

Finance

Finance is s wide-open field.

Some of the duties would include collections, accounting, record keeping for balance sheets, payroll, tax preparation, financial planning, retirement planning, and banking support.

Just about all industry sectors need this type of work performed regularly.

Customer Service

Customer service opportunities are frequent for freelancers who work well with other people.

Good people skills come in handy here. If you have the "gift of gab," you like dealing with the public, and can provide assistance in a kind and courteous manner, then this industry is for you.

Large and small companies are beginning to farm out this part of their business to work-at-home contractors.

This could include answering phones and directly dealing with customers for major corporations like retail establishments, online businesses, insurance companies, magazines, and newspapers.

Writing

Writing is another popular market that a freelancer could easily pursue.

A freelance writer's duties could include providing content for websites, blogs, newsletters, newspapers, magazines, and social media posts.

Writing also includes ebooks, ghostwriting, essay crafting, communications

consultant, copy editor, and brand analyst.

Education

Educational jobs would include training, workshops, and educational activities that extend beyond the classroom.

Target industries could include nonprofits, corporate entities, virtual platforms, and online schools.

Also, learning and education manager, language teacher, and hobby instructors all fall under this area.

Public Relations Consultant

Many public relations experts work as freelancers. These experts are considered self-employed.

This profession is sought after for political campaigns, bringing about education and awareness for businesses, politicians, nonprofits, schools, health departments, and schools.

Always keep a portfolio available to show proof of your previous work.

Transcriber

Businesses, lawyers, and media professionals have a demand for transcribing audio files. Having good typing, spelling, and listening skills are necessary here.

Graphic Designer

If you have an artistic flair and some technical knowledge, you could have much success here. Designers can design logos, websites, tee-shirts, billboards, flags, business cards, stationary, and visual brands for companies.

Virtual Assistant

Businesses need all sorts of administrative tasks taken care of, like monitoring emails, providing customer service, issuing invoices, and balancing the books.

Today, all these things can be done remotely online. Work as a freelance virtual assistant for one business or split your time between several.

Travel Consulting

If you enjoy traveling and helping others pick a destination, then working as a travel consultant is perfect for you. Many travel consultants work as independent contractors for larger companies and earn a good income doing so.

Accounting

Are you good at balancing money?

Then working as an accountant may be a good choice.

Many small businesses and organizations need help with their finances and balancing their books. If you are familiar with accounting programs, this could open the door to many remote opportunities.

Online Researcher

Are you good at surfing the internet to find answers?

Companies pay good money to have this service provided to them.

Online researching is a new segment in the freelancing field because people are always on the lookout for the latest information to assist them with growing their businesses.

Editing

Editing services are vital to all communication aspects of a business or entity.

If you have a keen eye for finding grammatical mistakes, typos, or have a good command for the English language, you can perform editing tasks.

This would include reviewing books, articles, reports, documents, and magazines. The sky is the limit. Proofing and copyediting are also functions of an editor.

The salary ranges around $53,000 a year.

Social Media Management

Just about every business needs to have an online presence these days, beyond a simple website.

Social media helps these entities engage with their customers and attract new ones.

This could take up a great deal of time, and most companies farm out this duty to a contractor.

As a social media manager, you would keep track of changes, conversations, monitor accounts, and create posts.

The goal of most businesses is to increase their social following.

Social media managers can make up to $80,000 a year on a freelance basis.

Getting Started

Setting up an online profile gets you noticed as a freelancer ready for business.

Each platform will usually ask for different information to create a profile, but for the most part, you will have to give your name or company name, contact information like a phone number and email address.

Then, the platforms will ask to give your area of specialty.

Having samples of your work or portfolio is helpful.

Upload this information along with a picture if it is required.

This is the moment of truth. This is where you put your best foot forward and tell potential customers what you have to offer and why you are the best one to do it.

Don't be afraid to put your shine on and boast a little about your accomplishments.

You may want to write this information on a separate piece of paper to fine-tune it before inputting it on the actual platform.

Most platforms are decent marketplaces with an ample range of freelancing gigs. Many cover just about every sector available. Some include flexible jobs or remote contracts.

Before acting on these platforms, check if there is a price involved.

Job Marketplaces

Here is a list to get you started on the many freelance marketplace sites.

SolidGigs

https://members.solidgigs.com/

This platform saves time and money from hunting down freelancing jobs instead of doing work. The website has its staff comb the internet to search for freelancing jobs to post and to weed out those undesirable listings.

This platform also offers a library filled with courses, interviews, tools, and templates to assist aspiring freelancers.

Fiverr

https://www.fiverr.com/

Gigs start at $5, but there is a series of tiers attached as options to increase the total price.

This website is a great way to start to build your portfolio and handle various client work. I personally like Fiverr because it allows for more exposure in addition to curating jobs on your own.

Upwork

https://www.upwork.com/

This platform allows freelancers to obtain work from clients all over the world.

Upwork has a large job site. They have over 12 million freelancers and an estimated 5 million clients. An estimated 3 million freelance jobs were disseminated each year from this platform.

Do your homework, though. You might have to lower your price just a little to beat out the competition and remain marketable.

CloudPeeps

https://www.cloudpeeps.com/

Once you have a few gigs under your belt and gain more experience, then look at Cloudpeeps. They are a high-end marketplace. Their clients are exclusive in various niches.

If you are accepted, you'll be building a relationship with a company that offers marketing, social media, and copywriting services. Try it on for size and see if it suits you.

Indeed

https://www.indeed.com/

Indeed scans the whole internet for jobs and places them on their platform.

It is user-friendly, particularly for remote work.

The website even has a feature that allows freelancers to search for jobs in their local area, too, and it's free.

College Recruiter

https://www.collegerecruiter.com/

Recent graduates and students may want to try out this marketplace, which caters to that target audience.

The website is a good one for beginning freelancers looking for jobs that offer more experience than perhaps pay.

Approach this as curating future work.

Freelancer

https://www.freelancer.com/

This website offers a large array of projects. Freelancer provides 8 free applications before there's a membership fee.

Project charges are a little different, where there's a commission charge between $3-$5 or 3-5% on these projects.

Guru

https://www.guru.com/

Guru is easy to navigate through and to display your experience.

This feature makes it easier for potential clients to see your profile.

Each day, the website displays a great number of job postings. Guru charges around 9% commission on all jobs granted to freelance members.

ServiceScape

https://www.servicescape.com/

ServiceScape offers a massive, global marketplace for contract workers with varying skill levels.

This company tends to focus on graphic design, writing, and translating as core offerings. They have an estimated 259,000 finished projects and an excess of 79,000 companies who use the marketplace.

Craigslist

Craigslist traditionally has been a great posting

website for selling various goods. There, unfortunately, isn't the security of holding buyers accountable in any given transaction as the other platforms boast.

Most people posting on Craigslist are usually looking to get work done as soon as possible. Craigslist also offers job listings in every major city in the country. Remote work is also featured in the listings.

Getting Paid

The next function to perform in getting started as a freelancer is to have a method of payment in place. Setting up profiles on freelancing websites is only the first step.

PayPal

Opening a PayPal account is just as important as your marketplace accounts.

Once you have navigated around the different freelancing platforms and job boards, it is time to secure a payment method. PayPal is typically the universal choice for obtaining payment from clients. PayPal also has an invoicing feature where you can list the products or services that the freelancer provided for the agreed amount.

The thing that I love most about PayPal is that it protects the client and the vendor in the business deal. Each party is held accountable for the transaction that should go favorably.

PayPal simple to use and is straight forward. Go to their website, complete the information page, and decide if you want to have an individual or a company account. Then input your banking information for the portal to link to.

It may take a few days for the company to verify your identity and your bank legitimacy in making small deposits for you to then confirm this action.

When setting up your PayPal account, you must have a working email address. The company also requires that you agree to and complete their agreement for service statement.

If you are sending a money request to your client, the client would have to have a PayPal account also. You can always go on the website to check to see if the request has been paid or not at your convenience.

PayPal now allows a subscriber to link payment to their debit cards or the one that the company offers. Payments are immediate. There is no waiting on "the check is in the mail" possible client excuses or the use of snail mail. Through this method, the freelancer doesn't have to give out their personal banking information to customers.

PayPal charges a fee of 3.4% or more on all transactions. People from around the world use this service because of its convenience. Most freelancing websites support the PayPal payment method.

PayPal offers a safe and secure fund transfers and purchasing system.

Using PayPal is very easy and reliable.

Support is available in the event any problems may arise, it is resolved promptly.

Payoneer

A recent alternative to PayPal has entered the scene- Payoneer.

https://www.payoneer.com

There "about us" page says:

"*Payoneer enables millions of businesses and professionals from more than 200 countries and territories to connect with each other and grow globally through our cross-border payments platform. With Payoneer's fast, flexible, secure, and low-cost solutions, marketplaces, networks, businesses and professionals throughout the world can pay and get paid globally, as easily as they do locally.*"

Once you create an account, you can link your banking information, similar to PayPal.

The services they offer to freelancers include:

- Get paid by leading marketplaces including Upwork, Fiverr, Getty Images, and more
- Get paid by your global clients
- Withdraw your earnings to your local bank account at low rates
- Withdraw funds at ATMs
- Pay your suppliers and subcontractors for free

While PayPal is more renowned, Payoneer may offer you a viable alternative, especially if you have many clients in other countries.

How to Draw Attention

There are some major ways to make yourself stand out amongst the sea of other freelances seeking the same thing in the same spaces you frequent.

A freelancer's profile is the first thing that connects you to the potential client.

This could be the determining factor in whether you land the job or are passed over for your competition.

Taking measurable action steps will help you get and secure more clients.

Learning to market yourself is the factor that determines your success or failure. The priority should be to set yourself apart from the others.

Create a Winning Profile

Let's start with a winning profile.

Since this is the primary way to secure business and earn a paycheck, remember to step up your game.

Labor reports predict that by the year 2020, nearly 40% of the United States workforce will contain freelancers.

Get Straight to the Point

Write a clear headline that draws attention. Then develop a title, state your years of experience, and define your areas of expertise.

Answer Question Words

Next, tell the who, what, where, and how of your offerings.

The devil is in the details. This means while something might seem simple at first glance, it is more complicated than expected and requires more effort.

For instance, explain how you were able to increase a former client's bottom line by implementing certain strategies.

Demonstrate in your profile, your qualifications, years of experience. Present links to your work samples.

Be Concise, Yet Thorough

Business people are busy and usually operate on limited time. State your case from the beginning, but don't present a lot of fluff to win the client over to do business with you.

Besides stressing the fact that you would be an added value to his or her organization, show them with past examples of your work.

It's a Resume

A digital profile is similar to a resume. Just like a resume, you would align your qualifications with the line items the potential client has laid out.

For instance, if you were an artist and the client wanted a mural painted, you could present in your profile the unique styles you have used in the past or are using currently that's proven successful with previous clients.

Use a Professional Picture

Upload a professional picture of yourself for your

profile page that resembles confidence and professionalism.

I always wear blue for pictures or important meetings. Blue is an inviting, nonintimidating, reliable, calming color that seems to win audiences regardless of the situation or circumstance. I don't call this superstition, but rather insightful.

Update as Needed

Once you've set up your profile, remember to provide continuous updates when necessary. Remind yourself to update your portfolio on all freelancing platforms.

Websites like Dribble and Contently serve as good reminders to perform this task regularly. Each time something new occurs in your work, add it to your portfolio.

For instance, if you have landed a major account or were lauded for freelancing accomplishments, post it on your profile.

My mother used to tell me all the time, "it's not what you say, it's how you say it." Meaning you can give yourself a pat on the back while exercising some level of tact.

Simply tell your story. Highlight the important aspects of the experience, which will help you keep and expand potential and existing clients.

Add new copy. Include up to date awards, certificates, and earned experience.

Connect the Personal

Remember to connect your personal and professional accounts to your freelancing platform. Pay attention to your online presence.

Since clients could very well examine your personal social media presence before deciding to hire you, monitor your personal accounts activity and beware of what you post. Put your best foot forward everywhere, because the entire internet is your workplace!

Charge Fairly

Determine a competitive rate of pay for your services.

Don't Undercharge

Do your homework and research what the going rates are for this type of service. What are your competitors charging for the same type of work?

Beginning freelancers may feel underbidding means winning certain contracts over a competitor. It is okay to underbid, but not to the degree that hinders and jeopardizes your bottom line in the end.

This means that it is okay to shave some of the cost to ensure a long-term contract.

Don't underbid to the point where it's not worth the trouble or costs more in terms of your time.

Don't Overcharge

With this in mind, be careful of overpricing your service as well. It is easy to lose a potential client due to overpricing services.

Again, do your homework and find out what your competitors are charging. What the standard rate is and what added value you bring to the table justifies your prices.

You can use experience in work-related gigs or mastery in a skill. They both work well when defending the cost of your services.

The 30 Day Challenge

What if I told you that you could make $1,000 in your first 30 days as a freelancer? In reality, if you could work on your freelancing work fulltime, you could potentially make even more!

Here's how I did it.

Examine Your Worth

Look at your current workload. Remove those items which pay the least amount of money per month.

You can handle this in two ways:

1. Convince lower-paying customers to pay more by offering additional services to them.

2. Ask for payment upfront from the ones who are paying the most.

This creates a positive cash flow. This means you're not tying up your money for some future day but rather reaping the benefits now.

To up the ante in my own experiences in raising capital, I have offered services at a discount rate for payment upfront. Most business people can immediately see the value of such an arrangement.

Getting the same services for a lower price makes sense to any client who is looking to get the most bang for their buck.

Reach Out

I then contacted five associates with whom I'd had previous conversations. At that time, we had discussed that they would be interested in my services once it was an affordable option for them.

I approached them with a proposal incorporating these desired services at a reasonable rate, and they were amenable to the proposal.

Word of Mouth is Gold

As I mentioned earlier, offering incentives to current customers for referrals is another great choice in increasing your bottom line.

I once did a media plan for a client that turned out to be a huge success. He told four of his closest colleagues about how he was happy with my services. Some of his friends that I had never met before were eager to sign with me. It was their trust in the friend's word that almost guaranteed the deal.

As I was conducting work for them, I asked all participants for referrals to contact or who they thought may be in need of my services. The idea was to depend on the fact that if I increased the client's bottom line, they would increase mine.

From that one client came 4 referrals and those 4 referrals referred other people, and before you know it, I had a stable, well-paying client base.

Network

Another great sure-fire marketing strategy is to network. Make a daily list of those potential clients in your niche.

Go to meetings where they are members or partake in activities that they indulge in. Take the opportunity to introduce yourself and what you have to offer.

I used to make it a daily task to contact those persons on the list with a phone call or in-person, leaving my business card and making the interaction as casual as possible.

Maintain your network. Continue to build your network and your freelancing brand. Keep in touch with clients, family and friends, and other professionals by meeting with them, sending emails to them, or simply to thank them.

Former clients are an excellent source for more freelancing work. Just making a phone call or reaching out to them to inform them of new successful projects you're working on and that that you would love to continue building a relationship with them.

Be careful not to spam on the internet with sales pitches or show up uninvited to a potential client's place of business without permission.

Keep communications light without the pressure of a hard sale despite your need or desire for the client's business. For every contact, make sure you ask them are they aware of anyone they know who may be in the market for the type of service you provide.

Remember, leave no stone unturned. My motto is this: "All things are possible because there are possibilities in all things."

Be Personal

Ask potential clients if you could have a few moments to speak at an upcoming function they are hosting or a group that they are affiliated with. These tactics go a long way in padding and lining your pockets with future leads.

I know that we live in a digital age, but making money the old-fashioned way with meeting people face to face, shaking hands, and developing relationships always works better than an impersonal email or text.

Other Tips for a Successful Challenge

There are a few tips and tricks to encourage you to maintain your momentum in your quest to become a successful freelancer.

- If you feel a little uneasy about naming a price, always give the standard consulting rate of $35 an hour to discuss the details of the service.

- If you're looking to make at least $1,000 a month, diversify your contacts. Include on and offline places.

- Most freelancers spend over 70% of their day hunting for jobs. Make the most of this time!

- Other ideas on procuring work could be to write an eBook on your niche or expertise and sell it on Fiverr or Goodreads.

- Come up with cute sayings about your niche and put them

on tee-shirts and sell them on TeeSpring.

- Create a website that includes affiliate links, sponsored posts, and AdSense ads. These are proven strategies that work!

- Diversifying your streams of income may be the most important message I can give you.

- Revisit your network of clients to see if there are any other services you could offer.

- Research what your competition is doing in the same niche and incorporate these elements into your businesses.

- Be sure to ask for referrals from every client.

Combining each of these ideas along with marketing on platforms such as Elance, Freelancer, and Guru will increase your chances one hundred-fold in making $1000 per month and reaching potentially a 6-figure yearly income.

Set up Google alerts.

This service will send you emails regarding news involving your niche. These alerts are vital in staying abreast of start-up businesses and organizations that may need your service. Initiate several alerts to cover all the tasks you perform.

Remain in constant communication with your clients.

Inform them of any work you have done since you last talked to them and new information on current projects you're working on. This action shows off your professionalism and may give these clients some ideas about more work assignments to offer.

Always be on the lookout for freelancing business.

Try contacting different larger agencies to pitch for work or partner with. You never know if they could need someone just like you to help them fulfill their workload.

Chronicle your social media links.

Be sure to add your social media channels to your profile page on freelancing platforms, your website, Twitter, and LinkedIn profile. This will make it easier for people to find you and build a following as well.

Ask for kind words.

Always ask for a recommendation or referral from potential and current clients. Word-of-mouth is the best marketing tool to get your name out there.

If your customers are satisfied with your work, ask them to give a testimonial and place it on your website, social media channels, and portfolio.

Stay in the know.

Stay abreast of all the new and latest training in your niche. Get the most updated news and tools while mastering each.

Brand yourself as an expert or authority in your area of expertise. This makes you a shoo-in when marketing yourself and giving yourself an edge up over the competition.

Building a solid reputation is important in the freelancing world.

There are several ways to accomplish this feat. You could connect with influencers in your niche.

You could write an ebook, design an online course, or line up some speaking engagements.

Hosting workshops and training sessions are also some solid ideas to show off your expertise at your craft.

Do case studies in your niche. These studies do not have to be elaborate but should show the ways you have enhanced your client's lives. Include statistics and any return on your investments.

Image is everything.

Remember to keep tabs on your virtual image. Be sure to check using Google alerts to scan the internet on anything involving your name or company name. Check to see if there is any negative information out there that may hinder you from getting work.

Perfect your niche.

Determine what your expertise should be. Decide what will be your focus.

Get listed on the search engines and directories. Go to Google to get the exact names of who to send your submissions to. Only send these websites up to date information on yourself.

Make sure these virtual entities are legitimate web pages.

Involve yourself with coworking spaces.

Freelancing can be a lonely experience, but it doesn't have to be.

Try integrating yourself and aligning yourself with co-working environments.

This can serve several purposes:

- It can help to stay motivated

- It can offer insight into the outside business world

- It can provide avenues for networking

Consider freebies.

Give free phone consultations that will help build your network of potential clients. This is called planting seeds for future work. While potential clients may not act on a proposal with you right away, you made an impression on them to consider in the future.

Partnering with other freelancers or people will increase your bottom line.

It is okay to work with others on projects. These people could complement your talent and develop a team that cements the deal.

Be careful to maintain your authority in this collaboration. You may even want to have agreements of noncompetition before any work begins to ensure everything goes smoothly.

Engagement is key.

Incorporate activities that engage with your customers. You could hold a contest for the first client to answer certain news trivia or send out newsletters or emails to your client base.

Keep them in the loop with your activities and the latest news within their niche.

Remember to send out personal birthday cards and well-wishes to your clients.

Buy ads.

Take out a small ad in a trade publication or local community paper.

Be sure that these ads would reach decision-makers in your target audience. Use AdWords, Facebook, and social media to accomplish this goal.

Write for niche publications.

Guest posts and blogging gives an excellent opportunity to show off your special skills.

Find out which websites offer writing opportunities, whether through blogging or guest posting, and contribute to them as often as possible.

This helps to build your following within your niche. LinkedIn groups and Quora are good starting places.

Carefully negotiate.

When negotiating a price, ask for the client's budget for the project first.

This allows the freelancer some wiggle room to increase or to decrease a set amount price. Most often, clients will want to find out how much the project will cost them before stating a price.

Beat them to the punch by asking them politely what type of budget were they thinking about before you offer an amount to do the work.

Refer to yourself as a consultant on the project.

Give the customer the feeling that you are professional.

Use the word "consultant" in all communications with the client. Also, always say "we" instead of "I," letting the customer think your work on his or her project is a team effort.

Adjust your prices.

Periodically increase your prices with current inflation rates. This is typically a standard rate of 5-10% annually. You can do this with new and existing clients on an as-needed basis.

The start of the year is a good time to implement this strategy.

Set boundaries.

It is okay to say no.

When you are a beginning freelancer, telling a potential customer no can be challenging. Saying no means you are getting a fair price for the services rendered.

Learn the art of negotiation. Read up on this or watch a YouTube video on the techniques of negotiation.

Never lower your price with the hope that your customers will continue to do business with you. **Get the pay you deserve for each project proposed to you.**

Place a cut-off time for your proposals to expire. When a potential client is genuinely interested, they will act on it promptly. Freelancers need a deadline to complete work and to get a response to a proposed project.

Communication advice.

Let the customer do most of the talking at your meetings. Just listen and take in every word or message that your client is giving out. You can then ask any questions or more clarification if necessary.

Be sure that you are interacting with the decision-maker at your client's office. There's no need to spin your wheels with someone who doesn't make the final decisions.

Gain all the info.

Short of carrying a tape recorder at every meeting with a potential customer, learn the art of speed writing to take specific notes on conversations with the customer. You can then go back and review them if need be.

Some freelancers carry around a tablet or some form of mobile device to capture the details of the contract negotiations. These things may not be spelled out in the contract, but you would have record of them, just in case.

Ask the customer what they are looking to achieve with the proposed project to avoid problems further along in the project. It may seem like an added amount of energy spent on this one specific aspect of the project, but the customers' expectations go a long way in terms of communications and, ultimately, delivery.

Send a contract for every sale. Lay out the details of the work you will perform for the client and any specifics on the project coming from the client. If the details are spelled out, it elevates the guesswork or attempting to recall certain information previously discussed.

Nearing the end of every project, ask the customer for feedback and what their experience was like working with you. Personal testimonies help other potential customers make the decision to sign on with you, hearing other people's opinions about you and your services.

Finance matters.

Set up a business checking and savings account. Most often, this will require a certain amount of money needed to open the accounts.

Think about incorporating your enterprise. This gives additional protection in case someone tries to sue you. You won't jeopardize your personal belongings and lose your shirt on a deal that went sour.

Accept various forms of payment. Most businesspeople never use cash as payment to vendors. Some of your customers will pay you with a check, credit card, or electronic transfers.

Ask for a down payment from every sale. Clients will respect you for this and feel that you are serious about getting down to business. Recommended down payments that can range from 30% to 50%.

Invest in automatic invoice reminders. It is easy to forget this important detail when you are busy fulling orders from clients.

Create a budget for yourself. Include any expenses that may arise while working on projects. Get the details of the actual expenses involved. Unexpected expenses are to be expected. Allow for this unknown factor when it happens. Prepare yourself.

As an incentive to clients for paying on time, **offer a discount and charge those clients for any late payments coming from them.** Adding an additional charge to clients that pay late will encourage them to pay on time.

Either **purchase bookkeeping software** to handle your books yourself or hire a bookkeeper to keep track of your accounting. Fees for this type of service for a small entity is typically nominal.

Establish a designated workplace.

Most freelancers have a home office where they work from. Every now and again, a client may request work to be completed from their office.

Selecting an area where all work is done saves time in having everything you need to complete a task right before you in one area. This is more imperative for freelancers also because all important papers and documents are at your disposal.

Having the proper equipment to complete projects is important. If you need a scanner or a printer to help with workflow or client demands, obtain those items to conduct the job proficiently.

Running around trying to find a place to copy material or to send a hard copy to a potential client for approval is time-consuming.

Time management skills.

Throughout your often busy schedule, always remember to make yourself accessible. Clients want to feel confident that you are available to their needs. Customers want to know for sure that they can contact you if need be.

Avoid burnout. Take the necessary breaks between assignments and current jobs. This will allow for greater productivity, rejuvenation, freshness, rest, and focus.

Stay on task and maintain a steady, adequate pace. It is easy to lose focus of time when you don't have someone looking over your shoulder watching.

Set realistic goals. Plan your day in advance and set milestones.

For example, schedule a certain amount of time to procure clients. Establish a goal to also completed work for a designated time. You can decide to contact at least 10 people a day to pitch for more business and to complete current projects.

Find mentors.

Search for mentors in your niche area. These experts have a tremendous amount of resources to lend and learn from.

These mentors could help you grow your network and obtain a steady stream of work from potential clients.

Look on social media to contact some of these individuals to assist you in running your freelancing business.

Get insurance.

Research liability insurance, particularly. Having insurance will provide a cushion for you in your business dealings.

As you are self-employed, you should also seek purchasing health insurance.

You have to provide your own benefits since an employer isn't doing that for you.

Conclusion

> **IF YOU HAVE A GOAL, BE RELENTLESS IN YOUR PURSUIT.**
> — Keith J Davis Jr

Most people fail not because they lack the know-how or talent in their industry, but rather because they quit trying.

"Nothing beats a failure, but a try" rings true in this instance.

I have attempted to support, ensure, and praise all those people in the world who seek to turn their dream of becoming a freelancer into a reality.

Freelancing involves work performed on a contractual basis for a certain agreed-upon price for a certain agreed-upon service. In a nutshell, freelancing is basically a form of self-employment.

Some wage-earners perform side work on a part-time basis, some full-time, depending on your risk tolerance as a way of making extra dollars on the side that can turn into a full-time gig.

Carving out a niche for yourself is the first step to acquiring a lucrative and rewarding career in the area of self-employment. Preparing to go after these goals can seem like a huge hurdle, yet the road gets a little smoother as you go along on this path.

Think about what talents you possess that people will pay you to perform.

Increase your bottom line by signing up with freelancing platforms and freelancing job boards.

Make a list of potential clients, starting with family and friends. Get them on board and gather referrals from people who may be in the market for your service.

Develop a list of potential customers taken from newspaper listings of start-up businesses in the business section of the local paper. Join groups and organizations in your niche. Contact everyone on the list and push your wares or services.

Freelancers can volunteer services to nonprofits sectors, perform public speaking, align with city and state agencies, to offer your niche at their events or monthly activities. Schools, training departments, and public housing agencies offer opportunities to expand your client base.

Join a speaker's bureau or rent out booths at major events, fairs, and bazaars. Obtain a list of convention events to become a vendor or attend to network and pass out business cards. Churches and places of worship are also a segment to tap into for freelance work.

The face of America's workforce is changing. Labor experts agree that freelancing or side-hustle is the new norm and is driving the economic wheel. Many freelancers earn a good, honest living doing this type of work.

Being prepared is crucial. Having a system of safety nets in place at the start will compensate for late checks, bounced checks, and underpaid checks. This could be the worst-case scenario. As you build your reputation among your target audience of potential customers, this tested system comes in handy.

Keep in mind that freelancing for a living is risky business, yet a rewarding one. Payments can be inconsistent as unexpected charges may occur while conducting your business, and staying on top of tax requirements is crucial.

Freelancers are a unique breed of wage-earners. They also have decided to enter into an open labor pool and chosen to seek an alternative way of earning a living. Yet, freelancers have been savvy enough to convince potential customers to choose them as their contractor of choice. Think before you leap. Get a hefty number of clients before you quit your day job.

Freelancers trade in their traditional work schedules for meetings in coffee rooms, restaurants, and libraries.

Most deals are signed through this method.

Still, seeking other ways of earning a living while juggling work and home life is an ongoing quest. Freelancing offers an alternative.

Let's make it clear. Freelancing is hard work too.

While freelancing is a unique form of labor, it is

considered work. Like working for yourself, the freelancer pays their own taxes, keep track of their time and labor. Freelancers are free to work just about anywhere, but most choose to work from home.

Keeping this in mind, you are officially considered a consultant. That is what it is professionally termed as when you bring your expertise to a client, and they pay you for it.

Becoming a successful freelancer is possible. Making this dream a reality is also achievable.

Equipping yourself with the knowledge, training, and resources will help jump-start your journey. Soon, you will be well on your way to a lucrative and rewarding career.

Thank you for reading this book, I love that you are interested in my life's journey as a freelancer. I am honored to share my experience and advice with you.

If I have helped you in any way, would you please leave me a review? I would sincerely appreciate any feedback you can provide.

 **Loved it**

Best of luck with your career!

www.ingramcontent.com/pod-product-compliance
Lightning Source LLC
Chambersburg PA
CBHW070805220526
45466CB00002B/558